From Spirit To Spirit

From Spirit To Spirit

A BOOK OF POETRY
BY
MINERVA L. WORD

authorHOUSE®

AuthorHouse™
1663 Liberty Drive
Bloomington, IN 47403
www.authorhouse.com
Phone: 1-800-839-8640

First published by AuthorHouse   11/10/2011

ISBN: 978-1-4634-8770-6 (sc)
ISBN: 978-1-4634-8769-0 (ebk)

Printed in the United States of America

This book is dedicated to my mother who was an inspiration and model for my life.

Margaret Ann Word—Reichman

11-12-1914 to 05-05-2005

MINERVA L. **WORD**

ABOUT THE AUTHOR

Minerva L. Word was born and raised in Chicago, Illinois, and now resides in Glendale, Arizona. Her education includes a BA degree from Roosevelt University in Chicago, MA level studies at the University of Chicago, MA degree in Supervision and Administration, and a second MA in English as a Second Language (ESL) from the University of Phoenix, in Phoenix Arizona,. She also holds a Secondary Teaching Certificate from Ottawa University, located in Phoenix Arizona and is now a high school teacher of World History and U.S. Government.

Minerva became a born again Christian in 1975. She then was given the gift of writing inspirational poetry, that you will experience in the following pages of *"FROM SPIRIT TO SPIRIT.*

Minerva believes that she has been given a gift from the Holy Spirit to write poetry that is healing. Poetry Therapy is not new, nor untried, but coupled with the Holy Spirit can truly ease life's burdens and renew the spirit in man.

This book of poems was written with you in mind. The challenges, pain, and sorrow experienced in life can work to the detriment of the human soul. The soul and spirit in man must be lifted and aided in order to sustain a quality of life while affording the soul an opportunity to be healed and grow into the image and likeness of the true Son of the Living God, The Father.

Souls will be healed, encouraged, and inspired while reading and meditating on these pages. Others have been healed and helped, and so can you. If you would have faith as a mustard seed, and believe. Some experience instant healings, and others experience slow evidence of a change and newness over a period of time in their daily lives. Come along with Minerva, and discover new life and a new quality of living, and know that there is hope and a way of living that is centered in the Living God that can liberate and restore your life. Let not your heart be troubled, let your soul freely experience the healing powers of the Holy Spirit as you absorb new life through Inspirational Poetry Therapy.

I love you writes the author, and this book represents that love. Minerva has faith that everyone who reads these pages will receive special blessings and encouragement to overcome all present difficulties and problems that they are facing in their lives. This book was written to glorify God the Father, and to allow man to realize that God is alive now and capable of answering our humble prayers. All illustrations were completed exclusively by the author to enhance the poetry, and to lend to each poem a feeling that truly the reader, the poet, and the Holy Spirit are one. From Spirit, to Spirit, to Spirit, writes the poet.

Footnote:

This book represents an accumulation of poems written over a long period of time. Ibis is a great accomplishment for me, to be able to express the Father's Love, and to be able to give them to you as a part of Him is truly a gift and a blessing. I give to you all my love and inspiration. May God the Father always walk and talk to you through these pages.

Thank You,

FORWARD

IN THE BEGINNING WAS THE WORD, AND THE WORD WAS WITH GOD, ANDTHE WORD WAS GOD. THE SAME WAS IN THE BEGINNING WITH GOD. In, 1:1

IN HIM WAS LIFE; AND THE LIFE WAS THE LIGHT OF MEN. In, 1:4

AND THE LIGHT SHINETH IN DARKNESS: AND THE DARKNESS COMPREHENDED IT NOT. In, 1 : 5

THAT WAS THE TRUE LIGHT, WHICH LIGHTETH EVERY MAN THAT COMETH INTO THE WORLD. In, 1:9

HE CAME UNTO HIS OWN, AND HIS OWN RECEIVED HIM NOT. BUT AS MANY AS RECEIVED HIM, TO THEM GAVE HE POWER TO BECOME THE SONS OF GOD, EVEN TO THEM THAT BELIEVE ON HIS NAME. In, 1:11,12.

I DEDICATE THIS BOOK TO ALL MY LOVED ONES, INCLUDING THOSE WHO SEEK TRUTH AND RIGHTEOUSNESS, MAY YOU FIND WITHIN THESE FOLLOWING PAGES, PEACE, COMFORT, AND THE LIGHT THAT CAME TO GIVE YOU LIFE MORE ABUNDANTLY. THE FOLLOWING PAGES ARE DEDICATED TO:

THOSE WHO LOVE GOD AND HOLD HIM NEAR.

THOSE WHO SEEK GOD THROUGH THEIR EARTHLY FEAR.

THOSE WHO BELIEVE THEY KNOW THE ANSWERS, BUT ARE NOT SURE.

THOSE WHO QUEST AFTER RIGHTEOUSNESS, AND WANT TO BE PURE.

JUST OPEN THESE PAGES AND READ WHAT I'VE WROTE.

TO YOU THE HOLY SPIRIT SPOKE.

CONTENTS

FATHER, I NEED SOMEONE TO TALK TO

Father, I need someone to talk to. How
shall I spend the rest of my life, in
poverty, or in prosperity? How shall I
find You and the peace You promised? I need
strength to carryon. This is the first day of
the rest of my life and I want to spend it
searching for truth, peace, prosperity,
Please: FATHER I NEED YOU————————

I KNOW YOU NEED ME. MY BELOVED, AND I AM HERE.
EVEN THOUGH YOU CANNOT SEE ME, I AM THE WIND ON YOUR
CHEEKS. I AM THE BREEZE BLOWING SOFTLY THROUGH YOUR
HAIR. FEEL ME, I AM HERE. SEEK ME WITH ALL YOUR
HEART AND SOUL YOU SHALL SURELY FIND ME. SIT
QUIETLY NOW AND KNOW I AM THE BREATH YOU BREATH AND
HEAR YOUR EVERY CALL. I KNOW YOUR NEEDS BEFORE YOU
ASK, FOR I CREATED YOU FROM THE COSMIC DUST AND EVERY
HAIR IS NUMBERED. PLEASE BELIEVE IN ME, AS I BELIEVE IN
YOU. HAVE JUST A LITTLE FAITH SO THAT I MAY WORK THROUGH
YOU TO OPEN DOORS THAT HAVE BEEN CLOSED AND FINALLY CLOSE
DOORS THAT NEED CLOSING FOREVER. I CAN DO ANYTHING, NOTHING
IS IMPOSSIBLE FOR ME, BUT I NEED YOUR WILLING CONSENT. YES
I KNOW YOU ARE SEEKING ME AND I AM SEEKING YOU SO THAT TOGETHER
WE CAN BE ONE AND SOLVE ALL YOUR PROBLEMS. I AM THE PROSPERITY
YOU ARE SEEKING, THE LOVE YOU ARE SEEKING AND THE TRUTH THAT
WILL SET YOU FREE. MAN'S DICTATES WILL HAVE NO AUTHORITY OVER
YOU FOR I AM YOUR FATHER FOREVER. COME MY CHILD KNOW THAT I
AM THAT I AM FOR I AM THAT WHICH YOU ARE SEEKING, I AM ALL TRUTH,
ALL THAT THERE IS NOW AND FOREVER. AMEN AND AMEN

THE FIRST DAY OF THE REST OF MY LIFE

This is the first day of the rest of my life
Let me live it dear Lord without strife:.
Give to me the peace I strongly need.
To replace the stress, to plant the seed
For yet another day lived with You
Jointly I know to conquer with true
Life lived as a gift, my life to renew
To continue the journey to the mountain top.
Too long have I struggled to find that its not
By struggling alone do we know when to stop
Because its not in the stopping and giving up
Do we learn to drink deeply of this earth's cup.
Let me rest my ~life in the bosom of peace
For the kingdom of heaven is not where we seek.
Please I pray and I know You can hear
Take away my burden, replace my fear.
Let me once again return to the child like grace
That I felt in this foreign place.
And when I forget my inheritance and gift,
Let me find in You my Lord Grace so swift.
Help me Lord this I pray, give to me one more day
So that I can be a house built on stone
Knowing no fear from the winds that have blown
Many houses down and were lost with the tide,
How can I fear dear Lord with You by my side?
Renew me in strength, renew me in mind,
Forgive my sins from the beginning of time.
I pray to You who promised to be near
And promised to love me and to always hear.
This is the first day of the rest of my life
Let me live it dear Lord without strife.

2

HANDS GENTLE AND STRONG

Sometimes when I feel all is lost,
And all is gone forever..
I sigh a sigh of deep emotion
That I think will sever
All the pent-up resignations
And all the lost dreams.
To renew my. soul forever to
Carry me down streams.
Streams that lead to life
Renewed to life more abounding
In hopes that were lost
Yet still life resounding,
. With what I know I can be.
Because my dear Lord You've
Made a heavenly place for me.

..

A place not made with hands like mine.
Hands that could change water to wine.
Hands that know no physical bounds •
Hands that were nailed at Calvery's mound.
Hands that washed away my sin and
Hands that loved every soul to win.
Sometimes when the world is near
And I am feeling blue.
Let me never forget, that
I've been held by You.
That all the lost dreams and hopes
That I felt were gone.
Were being carried by You dear Lord
With Hands gentle and strong.

CYCLES OF EVOLUTION

Evolving towards a perfect plan
Of God's relationship toward man.
Born of woman and cast down
How great thou art without a crown.
A little lower than the angels
Yet above and beyond the known,
Lost in doubt and enigma
You reap where you have sown.
Never to know or care once more
For priesthood side by side,
Never to morn for His face
From God our flesh subsides.
What do we know of peace,
Of peace beyond the norm.
Peace beyond the call of night
Within a Winter's storm.
Come my love, along with me
Where imaginations set you free,
Where soul and mind and longings meet
To tell of truth beyond defeat.
The healing of the soul in man,
The singing of his heart,
Cycles of evolution there, never to depart.

LORD FORGIVE MY SINS

How long have I displeased Thee
Lost in pleasures I do decree.
To converse with You pleadingly?
I say I am sorry and need Your Grace
But from Thee the next moment I hide my face.

LORD FORGIVE MY SINS

Father I am tired of earthly gain
For me You wore the scarlet stain?
Gleamed from Your Heart of sorrowed pain.
I am not worthy, not of Thee
Yet You've made a God of me?

LORD FORGIVE MY SINS

And when I give my life to Thee
Giving up all earthly gain.
Then and only then shall I be worthy
Of Your bright scarlet stain.
To heal and renew me once more
To renew my path to Eternity's shore.

FATHER YOUR GRACE ABOUNDS FOREVERMORE

AT HEAVEN'S DOOR

I came poorly to the Kingdom,
Not ready for the gifts that
Abound there at Heavens door.
Waiting with arms outstretched
Where Christians who got there
Before me the way was hard they knew.
They wiped my eyes, kissed my cheeks
And told me all they knew of the Glory
Revealed to them about the One they slew.
I set all my burdens down, all my cares
And woes, all my sorrows and my fears,
I gave to the One who knows.
A sense of peace filled my heart so strong,"
I could not stand, and yet I knew it all
Was real, it was all in God's Great Plan.

DIVINE WILL

I can't recall the time when
I felt the measure of life's thrill
Soon time will stand permanently still
And know I Thy Divine Will?

I remember youth in the Summertime,
How the ivy leaves would climb
Around about the window sill
Still know I Thy Divine Will?

I've looked in many a place, without
And know You couldn't be found about
Out there in the darkest night.
Still know I Thy Divine Will?

Then I searched within the halls of night
And searched with all my inner might.
I knew when I saw the inner glow,
Your Divine Will I began to know.

To share this faith. to proclaim your name
Before fallen man.
To study Your Word and live your life
To take a Godly stand.

As I learned meekly of You,
And of all Your Justly Ways.
Oh, my God Your Will be done
For the remainder of my all my days.

UNCARING

I know not why the rain drops fall,
Nor why the trees are green and tall.
I don't know why the clouds are gray
Nor why I bow my head and pray.
I only know that you are near
And close to me and very dear,
For every hair is known and numbered,
And where I lay my head for slumber.
And when my dreams are full of woe
You come to comfort me I know.
So I don't have to know the all,
For You are there if I should fall.
To pick me up, to start allover
For with You beside me I cannot fail
You sustain my life, You're my sail.
So on through life, I float on through.
Because I know my life is anchored in You.

"He Clothed the Lillies of the Fields"

FATHER I NEED YOU

Father, You said that You were love.
I have sought You, but all my life I
have not been able to find You. I have
looked for love everywhere, especially
from people, but they have just hurt me
causing me to flee from my suffering
away from them only to cause others pain
and sorrow in return. Where is the love
that I need to sustain my life and the
love I need to hang on?
Please: FATHER I NEED YOU——————.

MY BELOVED I KNOW YOU NEED ME, AND I LOVE YOU JUST AS YOU ARE.
MY LOVE IS UNCHANGING AND STEADFAST. IT IS NOT LIKE HUMAN LOVE
BUT WILL LAST FOREVER UNTIL THE END OF TIME, THIS I HAVE
PROMISED. FEEL MY LOVE, IT IS WARM AND SOOTHING. GET YOURSELF
OUT OF THE WAY SO THAT I MAY FLOW OUT FROM YOU TO TOUCH THOSE
IN YOUR WORLD AND FILL THEM WITH LOVE. I AM ALL THE LOVE THAT
EVER WAS, AND EVER WILL BE, YET YOU SAY I AM NOT ADEQUATE.
USE ME TO LOVE WHOM YOU CANNOT LOVE. ALLOW ME TO SHOW HOW AND
WHAT LOVE TRULY IS, A FORCE THAT CAN CHANGE ALL THINGS TO
REPRESENT MY OUTPOURING OF GOOD, PEACE, CHARITY. BELOVED YOU
HAVE LOOKED WITHOUT FOR THAT WHICH IS WITHIN, I HAVE LOVED YOU
BEFORE THE UNIVERSE WAS YET FORMED, I HAVE BREATHED THE BREATH
OF LIFE INTO YOUR BODY, SO THAT YOU COULD LIVE. I KNOW ALL
ABOUT YOU, MORE THAN YOU OR ANYONE ON EARTH WILL EVER KNOW.
YOU HAVE FORGOTTEN ME, OR HAVE NEVER CARED TO LEARN OF ME.
RETURN ONCE AGAIN TO MY HOUSE, YOU HAVE WANDERED FAR FROM ME
SO THAT I CAN FULFILL ALL YOUR NEEDS. COME REST AWHILE AND-_
KNOW THAT I AM EVERYWHERE PRESENT, I AM THAT I AM, I AM THE
LOVE YOU ARE SEEKING FOR I AM LOVE NOW AND FOR ALL ETERNITY.

NOT IN VAIN

Lord don't let me live in vain.
For that's the deepest sin of pain.
To squander all my gift away,
Is a horrible destiny I say.

For what if I die worst I be born
Long summers ago on that destined morn.
That You breathed the breath of life in me
And gave a part for the world to see.

A part of You in everything,
In the fields and meadows green.
And if I live for one more day,
Let it not be in vain I pray.

SEWING IN FAITH

The garment of Faith is woven fine
By threads not seen over periods of time.
In and out Faith weaves a pattern
Into what's seen in visible matter.

Know you or I what patterns we weave
When we ask Him for what we need.
He knows our needs before we ask
Because through Faith we create the task.

Believing in nothing the dye is caste
Turning our dreams into white ash.
So who's to blame when our life is spun,
Our dreams are gone, we've missed the fun.

Faith is based on things unseen
Woven in threads to a Higher Being.
Once a thread has been torn,
Wishes are lost before their born.

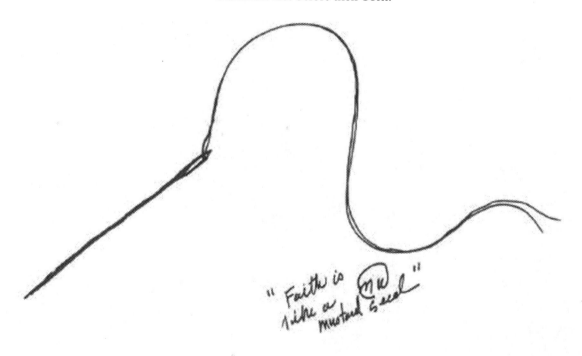

THE GIFT OF SALVATION

The gift of salvation comes from Christ.
You belong to Him, bought with a price.
Paid for in blood, truly an act of love.
He decided to love you in heaven above.

Believe that Christ died for sins.
Confess it to Him, new life begins.
Believe He is truly God's magnificent Son
Claiming for Himself all who were won.

For the gift of salvation all was paid,
When on the cross Christ's life was.l aid.
Down for all mankind to those who believe,
A gift freely given, sacrificed for thee.

Give your life to Christ and be born again.
Your life will be renewed, dead to sin.
Great and heavenly Father to Him pledge all,
Love for Eternity, redeemed from the fall.

Let us never wander far from Thee.
Gifts of the Spirit, for all to see.
Will always comfort and teach us to grow
Teach us to allow Living Waters to flow.

One day we will be in the likeness of You.
Who promised to finish the work began so new.
Great and Merciful God, thank You for the gift
Of immortal life, love, and Eternal sonship.

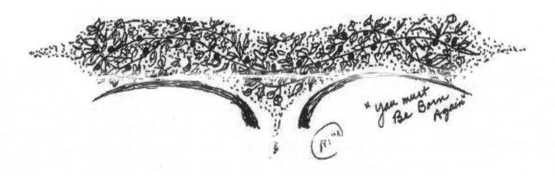

BE MY CHAMPION

When the fallen angel tempts me
With his lies and masked deceit,
And my life seems lost forever
Drowned in utter defeat,
Please dear Lord, champion my cause.

If in his arms I am lost
Tossed by storm and sea.
And the darkest night moves in
To engulf my will so subtly,
Please dear Lord champion my cause.

All his powers reign supreme
Over this world so wide.
No one can subdue him
For there is no place to hide,
Please dear Lord, champion my cause.

And when I said "I do believe"
Your blanket covered me.
From all dark powers of the
darkest lonely sea.

The fallen angel cannot stay
Cannot last because I pray
Dear heavenly Father
Champion my cause.

BY THE HOLY SPIRIT

Oh, Holy Spirit, Oh gift Divine.
Be mine forever, until the end of time.
Show me what service is, how can I please,
You alone are worthy, to fill all my needs.

Love me for all time, teach me Thy Ways.
Comfort me, instruct me, at your feet I lay.
Should I ever wander, far from your sight,
Great and loving Spirit, protect me through the night.

Place Thy word upon my lips, enclose it in my heart.
There to never leave me, never to depart.
Soon I will meet You, sooner than I know.
And then at Your feet I'll continue to grow.

I'll ask all the mysteries and longings of my heart.
Sweet Holy Spirit, how my soul will shout,
Praises to Your Glory, from a soul once lost.
I never could repay You, repay the cost.
For the bloodshed upon the wooden cross.

So take my life and hide it
In the bosom of your light.
Great and Holy Spirit while
In the long Eternal night.

HE DID IT ALL

I want to champion every wrong
And turn it into right.
And bring upon this earth
One day that's based on light.
And with this day I would herald
As one other before it could,
A resurrecting power,
Where darkness once stood.

But to the first was it given
This power to heal.
To us to replicate His deed
And in praise to kneel.

For the glory that He left
And power He had to raise,
All those that believe in Him
Through this earthly maze.

So my friends what can I say
This Poet so low,
But to remind you with this pen
He did it all you know.

SILENTLY

When I am touched silently,
My soul it knows the depth,
And God Himself stands witness
To thoughts inside I've kept.

Down through the years, I have known
The power of inner thought
To shape and form the world outside
As God Himself I sought.

And God in all His Wisdom
Knew me from the start,
Placed feelings in this soul
His love to fill my heart.

So when I am touched silently
By feelings and thoughts alike,
I know the perfect harmony
Of birds as they take flight.

For birds land on foreign soil
Their wings a tired thing,
But my thoughts return to me
My soul begins to sing.

God in all His mercy
Made a perfect way
For man to worship with Him,
To love Him and to pray.

In the regions of my mind
Where Spirit is born anew,
I am loved beyond all hope
Where fear His arrow slew.

SLEEP WILL COME

Sleep will come as I lay
All my burdens down
Upon my pillow rests my head
Sweet dreams they do abound.

The day has ended, all is well.
Safe in Thee I feel.
For my faith is in You,
My destiny to seal.
Give tomorrow as today
Love ever flowing.
Shed upon my soul,
Your Virtues, brilliant.
Ever glowing.

But most of all, If I should
Sleep beyond tomorrow's morn.
Take me up with You dear Lord
In Spirit to be born.
On wings like the angels,
In Thee I have no fear.
Please dear Lord carry me onward,
In Your light how near.
And when I reach that heavenly
Place where home shall be,
May I always worship and
Return my love to Thee.

JESUS GAVE ME ALL I NEED

Jesus gave me all I need,
For now and until forever.
Because of Him I know myself,
Lacking nothing ever.
Belief in Him, plants the seed,
Of life forever onward.
Builds the stuff that's called success,
And lets me know nevertheless,
That I am the branch, He is the tree
That makes me what I am to be.
Jesus gave me all I need,
For now and all Eternity

FATHER HARKEN TO MY PLEA

Lord this world is too much, too much
for me to bear. I want to come to You
so that I will be able to find what I
need to carryon, in my moments of sorrow
and pain, I need to know that You are there.
That You are here upon the face of the
earth to harken to my plea.
Please: FATHER I NEED YOU————

MY CHILD, I KNOW YOU NEED ME. EVERYDAY I HEAR YOUR CALL, I KNOW YOUR
EVERY NEED. REMOVE YOUR FEARS, AND FEEL MY PRESENCE. I AM THERE WITHIN
THE REGIONS OF YOUR MIND. BE STILL AND KNOW THAT I AM GOD. BECOME
ACQUAINTED WITH ME. RELAX AND KNOW THAT I AM WHAT I PROMISED TO BE
PURE SPIRIT AND NEED YOU IN SPIRIT TO WORSHIP ME. I AM READY TO ANSWER
YOU WHENEVER YOU YIELD YOURSELF TO ME SO THAT I MAY WORK THROUGH
YOU. FOR I AM LAW, OPERATING THROUGH MATTER TO EFFECT YOUR WORLD
BECAUSE YOU HAVE ALLOWED ME TO. I CANNOT WORK AGAINST THE FREE WILL
THAT I HAVE GIVEN TO YOU. I CAN DO ALL THINGS. WITH MAN THINGS ARE
IMPOSSIBLE BUT FOR ME NOTHING IS IMPOSSIBLE. LOVE ME, NEED ME, SEEK ME
WITH ALL YOUR HEART. SHARE WITH ME ALL THAT YOU ARE AND TURN OVER TO
ME ALL YOUR NEGATIVE EMOTIONS SO THAT I MAY PROVE MYSELF TO YOU. ONCE
YOU HAVE PROVED ME YOU WILL SEEK ME WILLINGLY KNOWING YOU HAVE HELP
INSTANTLY, WHENEVER YOU NEED IT. IF YOU LOVE YOUR PETTY JEALOUSIES MORE
THAN ME YOU CANNOT HAVE ME. KNOW THAT OMEGA. YOU WILL NOT BE ABLE TO
BLOW THEM AWAY, YOU WILL NOT I AM THAT I AM, I AM EVERLASTING. THE ALPHA
AND THE OMEGA

20

I COULD HAVE BEEN

I could have been a dog, a cat,
Even a large black rat.
I could have been a tree,
With branches flowing full and free.
I could have been a house
Standing on a hill.
Or a flower in a pot,
Upon a window sill.
But oh no, I look at me,
At the miracle that I see.
The life flowing in and out,
At the heart, strong and stout.
Thank You Father for Your Image,
Bestowed lovingly upon me.
A greater gift I could not have,
All through the long Eternity.

I BESEECH THEE

My soul is tossed by the prevailing sea.
The ugly tempest warring inside of me.
Still the storm, and raging waves,
That the Spirit silently braves.

The Peace that I have known so well,
Has left my shores and I cannot quell
The fury lying deep inside of me,
Of passionate emotions stirred unwittingly.

Peace, oh Peace, know I Thy face.
Peace that wandered from this place.
Return I beseech Thee in time,
When I am free of sin sublime.

Caress and hold me ever so near.
Though sin reigns, I know no fear.
Remain a lover of my soul,
Then inner harmony will unfold,
And Your Peace will follow me,
Please dear Lord, I beseech Thee.

NOT BY SIGHT

It seems we've come a long way Lord over many roads.
Along many byways with dark and dreary loads.
Along many sorrows to behold your face at last.
How shall we know You Lord, surely not by sight.
But by the leading of the Spirit in the inner light.

Renewed in mind, soul and body, let us never wander thus,
To give to the powers of darkness any power over us;
But by the leading of the Spirit in the inner light,
Let us advance slowly onward by faith and not by sight.

THE WAY OF THINGS

When the world seems dark and dreary I wonder why,
The heavens and earth were made and birds fly high?
What makes the sky so bright, why do clouds appear?
Why do stars come out, and the moon seem near?

There must be a God I think, or why all the fuss.
A God who created the Universe and made all of us.
A God without thinking, spoke through His need ~
Created the world we see, knowing what should be.

He created all the laws moving in perfect time.
Knowing man should think like Him. gave him a mind.
To create also, what his world would be,
Dominion over everything, land and sea.

So when I question the why of things,
My mind gives vent to vain imaginings,
And with an inner knowing, know why.
God creates as He is, a world for you and I.

FATHER FULFILL MY DESIRES

Lord they told me I had a disease
that I would never overcome. What shall
I do Lord? I don't want to be sick
and low in spirit and unable to do for
myself. Lord You said to ask believing
and You would heal me, that I had dominion
also here on earth. but I need You to show
me how to go about applying your laws to
fulfill my desires to be healed.
PLEASE FATHER I NEED YOU———

DEAR ONE, THE PAIN YOU FEEL HAS NO REALITY, FOR I AM ALL THINGS
GOOD, AND CANNOT BE OPPOSITE GOOD. PLEASE STOP BELIEVING IN
NEGATIVE THOUGHTS THAT BLOCK MY HEALING ENERGY. YES THEY TOLD
YOU THAT DISEASE IS A REALITY SO YOU BELIEVED THEM BEFORE ME,
PUTTING YOUR FAITH AND TRUST IN THEM, THUS IGNORING WHAT I HAVE
TOLD YOU FROM GENERATION TO GENERATION. YOU LOVE YOUR NEGATIVE
THOUGHTS MORE THAN ME, YOU NURSE THEM, YOU TALK ABOUT THEM AND
YOU COVET YOUR MISERY. REMOVE YOURSELF FROM NEGATIVE THOUGHTS
AND I WILL BE THERE. I LOVE YOU SO, AND I AM WAITING TO HEAL
YOU. COME TO ME MY BELOVED AND I WILL FULFILL ALL MY PROMISES.
FEEL ME NOW AS HEALING ENERGY, TOUCHING ALL THAT IS DISEASED.
I AM LIGHT AND IN THAT LIGHT IS NO DARKNESS. I AM SOOTHING
AND MOVE SLOWLY TO DISSOLVE ALL THAT IS OPPOSITE TO WHAT I AM.
RELEASE IT ALL TO ME, FOR I AM WITHIN THE MIDST OF YOU. TRUST
ME, FOR I AM THAT I AM, FOR I "AM THE HEALING ENERGY THAT YOU
ARE FEELING NOW.

"With God all things are possible if you Believe"

OF THEE

Lord if I had no eyes to see
Would I count my blessings so easily?
And how would I learn of Thee
With hope and faith, patiently?
Through the warmth of sun on my face,
The smell of flowers in this place?
How would I learn of Thee,
Of the power of Your Grace?

Through the winds as they blow,
Through the ice and feel of snow,
Through every gale and blizzard so,
Of You I think I would know.

Lord if I had no eyes to see,
Please my Lord stay by me.
Let the Holy Spirit guide me through
Life's sweet journey and all that's new.

For You I've learned are my eyes
We walk together side by side.
Lord if I had no eyes to see,
I'd count my blessings so easily.

COLLECTIVE THOUGHTS

CHILDHOOD

I remember those days dear Lord, it seemed I had all day to
play. The hours passed by as if in a dream and oh yes, I can
remember dancing freely in the rain I surely had all day long.
I never knew as You planned it Lord, how short an hour is and
a minute Lord is almost non-existent, and time is only relevant
to the now. A day was then like pages in a book, flipped and
one soon looses the page one is on. But no matter Lord, I only
pray that my days are the pages in your book of eternal life.

WE'RE HIS

If your way is not my way we are not divided, we are still one.
God expresses as he chooses, and you are to be free to express
His Life in a myriad of forms yet not thought of. Grow, maybe
apart, but still growth, not as I dictate, but as the Spirit
dictates. For you are on a journey in time and space. If your
road be not mine, take the part and go forward to your destiny.
For you are free to do the Will of God and your own thing as
the Spirit dictates. Who am I that I should dictate to you my
desires as to what you should do or be, am I God master of your
destiny? Somewhere we may meet again, our lives gently touching
and producing peace and harmony. Beauty is created as two souls
touch and feel a blending of the Universe. Corne, you and I
know there is no fear in being alone once again, as vessels.
Is there anxiety in knowing once again emptiness? Only in
emptiness extended over time do we fill up again, not with people
(who are empty within themselves) but with Spirit, Creative
Energy, to be what we were meant to be, Vessels for the Living God.

YOU NEVER PROMISED ME ROSES
IN MEMORY OF
GERALDYNE ANNJESS BOYD

(9-22-41 / 2-6-79)

You never promised me roses,
Nor a garden of daffodils.
The promises You made me
Were based on Calvary Hill.

Why do I therefore look for Thee
In places of earthly joy,
Knowing that my rewards are based
On burdens I learn to employ.

Help me dear Lord to see You
In every garden still,
Let me see You through eyes
That know of the Calvary Hill.

And when the roses fade,
As all roses must.
And the petals begin to fall
And whither away to dust.

Surely You'll be there
In Thee I've placed my trust
To carry me through the valley
Where petals never rust.

For the Truth has set me free
Released me from all sorrow,
Going to a bright new dawn
Based on a new tomorrow.

So to Thee Lord I entrust my all.
Knowing You've answered before I call.
Knowing I can have the roses and the daffodils
Because You made the sacrifice and died upon the hill.

FATHER SIN HAS A HOLD ON ME

Father, I have lived so long in sin, that it is as natural as
breathing. I am lost and cannot find my way back> to your
righteousness in Christ Jesus. Can You hear me, can You answer
my plea. Please Father redeem me from sin's hold over me, I
cannot. Increase my faith in You and Your promises.
Abba, FATHER I NEED YOU———

I AM HERE AS SURELY AS YOU SEE THE STARS OVERHEAD, I KNOW YOUR
HEART'S DESIRE. SIN HAS NO HOLD, THROUGH CHRIST AND THE HOLY
SPIRIT WITHIN YOU I HAVE ALLOWED YOU POWER TO OVERCOME SATAN'S
HOLD OVER YOU. YOU MUST TRY WITH ALL YOUR HEART. WITHOUT FAITH
YOU CAN DO NOTHING. I GAVE YOU A GREAT GIFT, THE HOLY SPIRIT,
WHO CAN OVERCOME ALL THINGS, I GAVE YOU FAITH, WHICH CAN MOVE
MOUNTAINS, AND WITHOUT WORKS IS DEAD, WITHOUT FAITH YOU CANNOT
PLEASE ME. COME MY BELOVED HAVE FAITH IN THE PROMISES THAT
I HAVE LEFT IN MY WORD FOR YOU TO FOLLOW. THEN SURELY YOU WILL
BE ABLE TO BE MORE THAN A CONQUERER THROUGH CHRIST JESUS. SIN
HAS NO HOLD, THROUGH CHRIST I HAVE ALLOWED YOU TO RETURN TO
ME. COME TO ME SO THAT YOU CAN FEEL AT PEACE, CLEANSED AND
FREE. THE DEMON WOULD HOLD YOU FOREVER, CAST DOWN, IF YOU GIVE
HIM POWER OVER YOU. BUT, HIS POWER HAS BEEN BROKEN FOR NOW
AND FOR ALL ETERNITY, IF YOU BELIEVE THAT IT IS. STOP SINNING
AND BE INSTANTLY ONE WITH ME, FOR I AM HOLY AND RIGHTEOUS.
I AM THAT I AM, I AM YOUR RIGHTEOUSNESS IN CHRIST JESUS NOW
AND FOREVER.

"There is no condemnation in those in Christ Jesus"

WITHIN ME

I have it within me to take a stand.
That takes my ship to a foreign land.
I go to the helm, I master the sails.
To lend a hand when all else fails.

For what am I but flesh and blood, a heart and mind
I take the course set for me, my eyes are blind,
To the Spirit that I feel, deep inside my soul
That leads me beyond self, onward toward the goal.

That I've set for myself, let no man know.
For dreams to come true, they must forever flow,
Upon a world where dreams come true, and are alive,
Because a Grace was given me, deep down inside.

Come, we all have within us, the power to know.
How to command our destinies and how to grow.
To create the world we want as down the path we go.
Knowing that for all Eternity, as above, so below.

A ROSE PETAL YOU ARE MOTHER DEAR

IN MEMORY OF EDNA P. JOHNSON

9-27-1900/6-1-1991

Have you ever seen a rose petal at the break of dawn?
or heard the melody of a new born song?
Or wondered why the sky is so blue
or seen the sea, a tidal wave or two?

Yo~ mother dear remind me of these
My hand in yours mom under the trees .
Stories you read, the laughter you brought
I remember mom, the lessons you taught.

I think too of the things you did,
To tickle my ribs and how I slid
Out of many a whipping, and oh yes,
I remember also, I was one big mess.

I remember apple pie, sugar and sweets
Hot roast beef and boiled vinegar beets
And also how you rolled out dough
And how your slim fingers could make a bough.

But above all I remember when
I felt your sweet kiss upon my chin.
Surely a rose petal could never be
As beautiful a rose as you are to me.

UNCARING

I know not why the rain drops fall
Nor why the trees are green and tall.
I know not why the clouds are gray
Nor why I bow my head to pray.
I only know that you are near
And close to me and very dear,
For every hair is known and numbered
And where I lay my head for slumber
And when my dreams are full of woe.
You come to comfort me I know.
So I don't have to know the all,
For You are there if I should fall.
To Pick me up to start allover
For with You beside me I cannot fail,
You sustain my life, You're my rudder, my sail.
So on through life, I float on through.
Because I know I am anchored in You.

STRANGER IN THE STREET

Angels cried when they saw a beggar in the street.
And cried even more when a stranger he did meet,
Who gave freely for the giving, the beggar had no feet.
The stranger had the Wisdom to see,
But by the Grace of God, that beggar was he.

HOW THE WORLD IS

I see how the world is,
its sadness, grief and sorrow.
I see how the world is,
based on hatred's tomorrows.

I see also the masks of men,
lost in the soul's desires.
Desires of all the lust
that the heart sires.

The negative and the hatred,
the prejudice and the pain,
all based on man's living
within the year's gain.

It can be no other way,
the goodness only parts
the darkness of night
hidden in men's hearts.

I see how the world is,
and yet I know
God's plan is also here
and love is also near.

When a tear falls
and a heart is healed,
God's plans are working too
in hearts that are sealed,
healing torn and damaged pain.

Yes, I see how the world is,
and I begin to know
If not for God's love
life would cease to grow.

What am I if I am not
here for all concerned.
I know how the world is
because I know God lives.

He lives within the heart of man.
Within the shadows there,
and I know without a doubt
That Love we are to share.

I know how the world is
evil abides here,
along with the good,
God is always near.

Without the light of morning's dew
and without the morning's glow
I would not know the world
darkness would prevail.

Souls would be lost
forever in lasting night.
The world would loose its living
would be without light.

I know how the world is
because I've seen the hearts of men.
Thank you heavenly Father, for your
Grace that abides within.

Making the world blessed without any
fear, worry, or fret, sorrow, or sadness.
Because of You Dear Lord have filled our
tomorrows with hope and gladness.

So I know how the world is, I also know of Thee.
Where You and angels await, at heaven's gate.
I live out my days here as many men do,
the only difference is, I live my days through You.

I WILL COME FOR THOSE WHO PRAY

Come talk to Me for awhile.
Let Me hear your words.
What would you have of Me?
You can have what you can see.

Before you asked for nothing.
Your faith was yet anew.
Believe in Me, and know
That day your sin I slew.

Let me wipe away your tears.
Let me fulfill your dreams
On the cross.where I hung
My love wiped out your fears.

Follow Me for all time.
Peace I leave behind
I go to the Father
The Spirit will be My sign.

So know My voice my children.
Know My Will for you.
Love is the key to heaven
Love makes all things new.

And on that day you see Me.
Descending in a cloud.
Your faith will be rewarded
As voices shout out loud.

"God Keeps His Promises"

Jesus in all His Glory.
Kept His Promise this day.
Touched the world as He said.
I come for those who pray.

Dear Heavenly Father,
Hallowed be Thy name.
Thy Kingdom come Thy will be done.
For all not just for some.

So keep on believing
Believe with all your might.
I will come when most sleep
carry you through the night.

DREAMS STILL UNDREAMT

When I was a little girl
And I became depressed,
I would climb inside my
Bed and I would take a rest.
A rest from the world outside
the worries and the fret,
To let my soul run free
In dreams still undreamt.

For in dreams I could find
Inner solitude.
Peace would come and I could
Find inner fortitude.
In valleys deep with
Daffodils I could run,
And clouds thick with dew
From a bright new sun.

Where my dreams would come
True without any thought.
And I became master Poet
For my dreams brought.
Hopes and wishes close to me
As only dreams can do.
And I dreamt for myself a
World where dreams come true.

PEACE

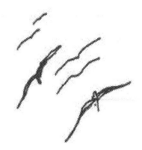

Peace is like a tidal wave,
Calm after the rush.
Like a tornado's aftermath
Blown to a hush.
Without knowing worry,
Peace cannot be found.
Without a loud noise,
What is sound.
And the peace that you seek
Will be eternally known,
Once you become humbled
And Spiritually grown.
And then the mind like a lake
Will mirror only peace.
Will reflect what you are
To a world that will seek,
Peace at any cost.
Peace beyond all measure.
Until then we wait patiently
For peace that will last forever.

WITHIN ME

I have it within me to take a stand.
That takes my ship to a foreign land.
I go to the helm, I master the sails.
To lend a hand when all else fails.

For what am I but flesh and blood, a heart and mind
I take the course set for me, my eyes are blind,
To the Spirit that I feel, deep inside my soul
That leads me beyond self, onward toward the goal.

That I've set for myself, let no man know.
For dreams to come true, they must forever flow,
Upon a world where dreams come true, and are alive,
Because a Grace was given me, deep down inside.

Come, we all have within us, the power to know.
How to command our destinies and how to grow.
To create the world we want as down the path we go.
Knowing that for all Eternity, as above, so below.

NIGHT SONG

Night songs gently in my ears
Bring haunting memories
Of life's forgotten tears,
Forgotten long ago, and lost
In memories flight.
Brought slowly to consciousness by
Crickets humming in the night.

When did the years go by, suddenly
I find myself old.
And just as the years passed,
My life became cold.
Leaving nothing to be desired,
All passed away.
The joy of youth left my lips,
As down the cricket's song!

And what was it all about,
This humming in the night.
Sung repeatedly in my ears,
By creatures without light.
I tell you that the darkness
holds no mysteries,
For I shall meet it soon enough.
When my soul this earth leaves,
To wander aimlessly the chilly, darkened night.
As my soul blends slowly with the creatures without sight.

SEASONS GONE BY NEVER DIE

Summertime is gone again
Leaves fall slowly as before,
And will continue to do so forevermore.
Autumn rises triumphant, sure
Bringing an array of color so pure.
Orange and brown, red and gold,
Will cover the ground ever so bold.
Winter is next, chilly and cold
Not like Autumn and colors of gold.
white as down, freezing wet,
Dies when Spring comes and yet,
Spring with it's power to awaken life
That was buried beneath the snow
knows the secret',. of the Universe
And how the life force begins to flow.
Never to die, nor cease to be,
Forever moving toward it's own destiny

TRUE AND GOOD FRIEND

I have known through
The years, many people who
I thought I loved and
Trusted but know I never knew.
Could never know them at all,
No matter how I tried.
And through the years,
Silent tears, how my heart cried.
But as a friend you were different,
Different from the rest.
Stood a head taller.
You were one of the best.
Good and true, sound and sure,
Friend in every way.
Now I take my turn in life.
Now I just must say.
Stay my friend, by my side,
Until the very end.
That you my friend will be there,
On that I can depend.
And I will remain true to you,
Through the thick and thin.
You're special to me my friend,
My love you sought to win.
And also remember through it all,
As the years dwindle down.
Friends never say good-by only,
"I'll be seeing you around".

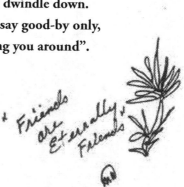

WISDOM IS

Wisdom is as Wisdom does, for Wisdom can't be seen.
Wisdom echoes forever onward and that would mean,
That Wisdom grows with time and that would seem,
That Wisdom can be partly sensed as in a night's dream.

What then do we know of Wisdom, which grows with time?
This ceaseless knowing, growing into eternal Mind.
Wisdom is not a respector of persons, knows no name,
But he who possesses Wisdom blossoms into fame.

Wisdom cannot be found in any given place,
Nor can Wisdom reflect it's beauty in a single face.
For Wisdom flows freely, pure and chaste,
From a fountain of Spirit upon the human race

"For Wisdom
ask of God
Freely"

INDEATH'S SHADOW

Death silently touched her cheek,
A friend of old, she did not seek,
Came in a moment and stood beside
Her shadow, there was no place to hide.

A friend of old, she did not weep.
Lost in sorrow, memories to keep,
Of lives lived, dreams dreamt,
And sorrows gone, all spent
On tomorrow's greatest, glorious dawn.

Death, where is thy sting?
An arrow only life can bring.
And surely all of us will feel
The anguish of thy blade of steel.

Come, my heart cries for loss of words,
That my spirit in sorrow knows
For friends that embraced your arms about,
Kissed your lips that without
That one final kiss, that one final embrace
Would never know freedom from this horrid place.

And yet, to go where souls are instantly free.
Where minds are all that can be.
Where prejudice and hatred have no place,
Where tears and sorrows know no face,
Where hearts love freely and embrace
In pure light, there is no trace—of pain.

So when death in my shadow kisses my lips.
May I kiss back fervently, eager to slip
Easily to the other side—in faith.
Released to the glow of existence without strife
Knowing I was created for eternal life.

THE ENCOUNTER

My friends know me, I them.
They recognize me slowly,
What remembering does send.
Friends aren't made, neither ·born
As in a dark dream, a memory forlorn.
Friends know me, a warmth appears,
That existed for many long years.
A recognition, long before we know
Which way to awaken, ever so slow.
As yet in a sleep, walking,
Speaking, saying "hello".
To continue some subconscious
relationship created eons ago ••
I tell you, my friends know me
long before I even say "hello".
Our lips parted and words started
The relationship began to grow.
For good or bad, how sad, for what
Are enemies but friends lost.
A bad encounter, a bridge to cross
A working out of destines, friend or foe?
As we evidently parted long, long ago.
By being free Spirits only then can we see
That friendships grow and will always be
Never parting, steady and Eternally free.

TRULY ONE

Mind and Time are everything.
Into my life they can bring,
Life more abundant, Life renewed.
Through Time itself the Life I knew
Was all Eternal, and Time itself flew.
Where to, I do not know, do not care.
I lived my gift, I do not dare
To pretend to know why or how,
Only that I gave my total all
To the gifts of Mind and Time.
To recall on occasion that I loved,
Cried, hated, felt numerous feelings
In a second of Thought, Thought the
Little sister of Mind, can conjure up
Anything and everything and can cut
Into the quick of Thinking instantly,
Bringing with it, it's cousins, feelings
Who are responsible for stealing from
Me all that I possess in the form of Peace.
But Time itself, I call and beseech
To rescue me from feelings, I cannot reach,
And to release my body from feeling's hold.
As I exert authority over my body so bold.
I learn to control all that I am in time.
To leave sisters and cousins of Mind behind.
Only then can I live freely, without doubt,
God, Spirit, Time, Mind, as within so without.

"Life is a gift lived by me"

OH! BEAUTIFUL WOMAN
INMEMORYOF
MARGARET ANN WORD-REICHMAN

11-21-1914 TO 05-05-2005

Oh! Beautiful woman so precious to me.
I love every part of you, the part I can't see.
For I'm an extension of you, what you've made of me,
Will honor you through time for the world to see.
You've carried me on your back, a burden so long.
It's time now to rest, let me sing you a song.
A song I will sing from the bottom of mY'heart,
From the bosom of my heart it will well up and start.
Oh! beautiful woman, you've sacrificed so,
To be a mother to me, to fight every foe.
Come to my bosom and rest your head,
Climb on my back and let me carry you instead
For I understand you now as never before.
You've opened my eyes, you've opened the door.
You've set a pace that many can't share.
You're the only one I know that really did care.
Thank you now from the bottom of my heart,
For standing beside me, for remaining a part
Of our love from the beginning of time.
Oh! beautiful woman, thanks for being mine.

FORGIVENESS

F—Is for Forgiveness which starts with me.

O—Is for Owing my heart freedom to be.

R—Is for Reasons I have buried inside.

G—Is for God who opens the door wide.

1—Is for Ignorance, not knowing how.

V—Is for Victory, I can overcome now.

E—Is forever, Eternally Free.

N—Is Never lost while in Thee.

E—Is Everyone that I thought evil of.

S—Is Sympathy for lack of love.

S—Is for the Sacrifice You made from above.

WAITING

When my plans are laid astray.
Laid to rest for another day.
Let not my heart be weary, neither be dismayed.
For I wait on Thee dear Lord, let my fears be stayed.

I rest dear Lord knowing Thee
Has hearkened to my desperate plea
To one day fulfill through me
A better tomorrow for all to see.

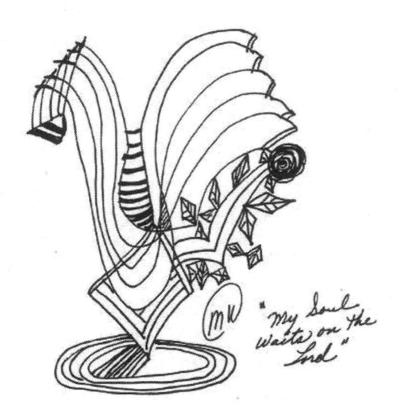

JOURNEY

I once viewed the world through rose tinted glasses .
Love ran thick then as sweet as sugar molasses.
Nothing was impossible, all was easily had,
Because I was creator, for my good or bad.

We all are didn't you know, a creator of sorts.
We send our ships out to new and misty ports.
To return some never again to remembered shores
But—pressing forever onward to unlock many doors.

Some ships are lost at sea amid torrent rain.
Some ships never leave port because of unknown pain.
Some ships float easily through the gallant sea of life
Yet other ships are banked because of unknown chartered strife.

What shall it be for you, flung into the open sea,
Know and remember you create your own destiny
At port, or on the sea, or on a distant shore,
You are the Captain, you plan the course, now and forever more.

THE BEGINNING

Soon the day ends and the night begins.
Over and over, again and again.
Never ending, complex but secure,
In knowing, if knowing is any surety
That tomorrow goes on and on
For all time, away never ending.
Forever moving upon a restless day,
Lost, therefore saved, but by whom?

You and I know that not even in
The tomb can we know, nor before in
The darkest womb, onward in journey,
Lost, gone forever in a stroke of
Longevity and lost hope. That the
Beginning was actually the end
And the end only the beginning.

PLEASE WAIT FOR ANOTHER DAY
(WE LOVE AND NEED YOU FOREVER)

How could you decide to end your life with one selfish act.
For you only prolonged pain this is an established fact.
Who are you to take your life away from those who love.
To leave an empty whole where there once was a living soul.

Sweet love, sweet love, made bittersweet by memories past.
For only memories can tell of your life lived to the last.
I wish we could have spoken more, spoken of your sorrow,
To help you change your life for a new and brighter tomorrow.

If you would have allowed time to heal all your inward troubles
You would have seen your worries blown away like bubbles,
To allow you again to live your life, to grow forever strong,
Here on earth is where you live and where you actually belong.

All your thoughts were filled with pain, joy you seldom knew.
You are Eternally free, because your loved ones prayed for you.
You now know how to face tomorrow, for you can surely see,
Every tomorrow was destined for life, for you and also me.

Your life cannot be wiped away, the hurt is left behind,
To haunt all your loved ones, to them please be kind.
Please wait for another day, forget thoughts of suicide.
Remember to live for others, you surely don't want to die.

We love you now and forever, yourself learn to forgive.
Love yourself and remember, you truly want to live.
Return once again to life, love and a bright tomorrow,
Based on a soul healed of pain, all sadness, and all sorrow.

THOUGHTS THAT ROB

When you have negative thoughts
That rob you of your peace.
Think clearly and see their just
Thoughts, and they will surely cease.
Separate thoughts from feelings
The two are not the same.
The lion that walks unhampered in
Thought will eventually become tame
To leave you free to be yourself
.. Upon this great earth plane.

"For Freedom
Christ has
set us
free"

STAINED

I saw a man with a tear,
Tatooed upon his face.
A tear it was near his eye,
A memorial to his anguished cry.
A soldier he was of foreign wars,
Of Vietnam I think.
He showed the world a living
Token of a ceaseless blink.
Of darkness and sorrow,
His soul could only tell
Of many months of terror
Spent in the bowels of hell.
Death leaves a mark within
The sad pitted eyes,
Of gory and bloody epitaphs,
This the mind denies.
But we know above all else,
America the Great,
Has built it's history
Upon souls gone by,
And all those who wait.

AN ETERNAL STORM

Jealousy is an emotion that
Leaves a crimson stain,
And replaces empty space
Where love has once lain.
Jealousy will steal and
Lie and yes even slay
To keep you forever,
Just to have its way.

Jealousy is dark and evil
Born of unnatural lust.
And shall never die
Erected in eternal dust.
If not held at bay
Jealousy can and will
Destroy cities and towns
And the heavens it will sway.

Jealousy cannot stand
Forever on its own,
It needs to be fed
From an eternal storm.
Then and only then
Can it be complete
To turn many innocent
Hearts into utter defeat.

IN PASSING

Tomorrow has yet begun and
Today is still upon me.
Yesterday all was spun
On the new day that was won.

Which is greater of the three?
Surely yesterday you will say.
For today is not finished
And tomorrow is far away.

Yesterday at one time stood
In tomorrow's place,
And today blended slowly
Leaving but a trace.

So you see today is great,
And tomorrow today will create
Yesterdays which are gone, however,
Creating an eternity spun forever.

A ROBIN'S SONG

I heard a robin sing today
In a very special way.
Full of life's expectations
For Spring was here to stay.

Everyday should be like Spring
Bringing newness of life.
Expectations should we have
Joy instead of strife.

Every minute, every hour
We too could sing,
To reinforce our life with power,
That newness would bring.

Should our days be dark and dreary,
Our souls burdened down.
No robin's song could we hear,
No rainbow to be found.

Lift up your eyes to the sun,
Your Spirit to the light.
Let the darkness part from you,
As the day from the night.

Come laugh awhile, and smile upon
All your sorrow too.
For Spring has come as the dawn,
When Christ came to you.

A VOID

I feel a void that many do
That nothing can fulfill.
For life and love and memories
Are laid upon a sill.
Where can I find once again
The many joys I knew.
That made my life worth living
The days away they flew.
And this void I cannot tell,
I don't know why it is.
I know it exists as part of me
Because I feel it is
But, because I feel it is
doesn't make it—so.
Just like I feel it for this moment,
It will surely go.
Another feeling will replace it
As before I know.
As the day follows night
I reach a certain height.
And the void once again
An old friend I feel,
Takes it's turn inside of me
Upon this endless wheel.

"When I am
weak, he is
strong"

LIVED

Life is a gift lived by me
Of love, hope and reality.
Life is a gift I surely want
The joy itself is enough to haunt
Me into believing the mysteries
Of life lived fully from this cup.
Life is a gift to be sure.
A gift I know that could lure
The best of us onward toward the goal,
Toward more life and beauty untold.

Why don't you try for just one day.
To apply the gift of life, just say.
Give me all and more than most
Of sweet life to live, a royal toast.
Lift my head and raise my sight.
Take the darkness from the night.
And if I should fail, so what!
I knew the sweetness of my cup.

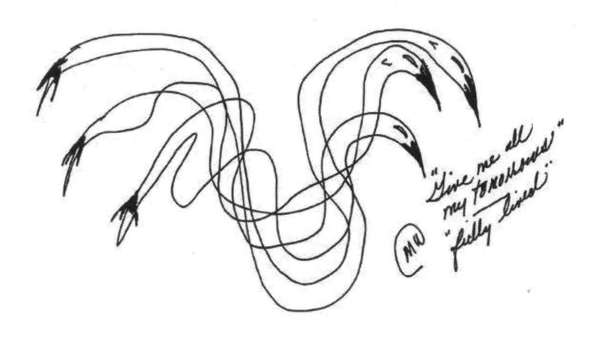

A WORLD BRIGHT AND NEW

I wish we all could dream
Our world bright and new.
Where misery and suffering
No man knew.
Where peace beyond imagining
Was every man's state,
And the world was full of food
And every man ate.
Where hate and bigotry did not exist,
And abundant blessings man could list.
But that would be paradise
And not the world we know.
Why must we die to find
Peace is just a state of mind.
Oh Man! oh creature who struggles so,
Who struggles past tomorrow.
Only to_ dream your dreams
Of life upon today's sorrow.
Victory goes to those who wait,
Wait patiently upon tomorrow.
For faith comes with the dawn,
Full strength gained from sorrow.

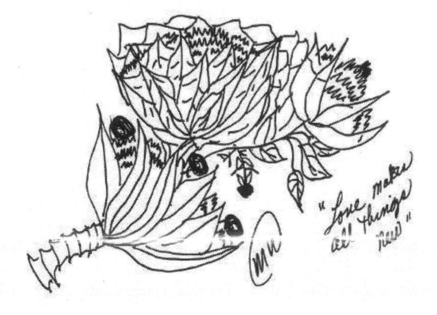

FRIENDS

I've lost friends in the past few years.
Was it me or them I now shed the tears.
I can't understand where I failed them so.
Was it a lack of understanding related so slow?

It was I think a growth of some kind,
Of spirit, of soul, physical or mind.
Standing proud in ourselves to make the choice.
To shout to the world, "I was right" and rejoice.

But in the quiet of night, when all is still,
A slight tugging in the heart that memories won't fill.
A part in the road, did I take the wrong turn?
Come back to me friend, something unquestioned I did not learn.

Interaction with you could have showed me the way,
Brought light through eternity who's to say.
But fear caught me up and my ego stood proud.
It's you not me, I shouted out loud.

But like a child who cries in the middle of the night
Who's afraid of the shadows left by your light.
Say you're sorry I beg you before it's too late.
I can't say I am sorry, I can't even relate.

"Friendship is love"

TIME MOVES ON

Time itself seems to pass
Ever so quickly on.
And yet I know and I feel
Time never stops upon
Anything nor anyone who seeks
To find out why.
Never ask nor never seek for
Time is but a cry.

A cry that can only be sensed
And yet we know it passes us
By constant changing events.
Events are the sister and brother
Of time, and move swiftly on.
Time doesn't care if you follow her
Or look back to find her gone.

One thing you'll find of time
As so many do.
Whatever games you've played,
the game will be on you.

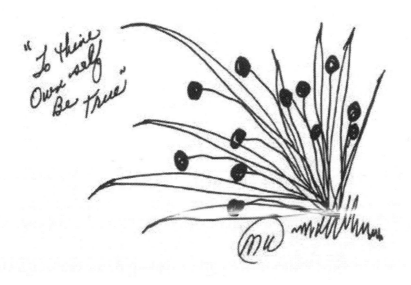

CAPITAL PUNISHMENT

A SIN

Thou shalt not kill
And take another's life.
For that life is lost
And full of human strife.
We are our brother's keeper,
Keeper of the faith.
God in all His Wisdom,
He made no mistake.
We put our flesh before God,
Knowing our vengeance will make
Us satisfied in promises kept,
Satisfied in tears wept.
So we pretend to be justified.
Christ was justified, we are inept.
He allowed the killing,
He didn't intervene,
All was known by Him, all was seen.
He allowed it all, can't you see,
To make us the Spirits He wants
His own to be.
Lacking vision and faith in Him,
We decide to kill,
Using the worldly system
A pain inside to still.
What is it with you, OH MAN,
Judging and being judged.
Taking Christ from the cross
Filling hell with the loss
Of those souls that would be redeemed
By Christ the promise that was foreseen
For all who have murdered
With a story to tell.
God forgives murderers, if they ask,
But we can't forgive our brother
A monumental, forgiving, loving task.
Satisfaction in killing another?

Abel you know was our brother,
Yet God did not slay Cain,
Through his seed another came.
Murder is murder and
Capital Punishment a sin
No matter what the circumstances
We find ourselves in.
Father in your infinite Wisdom,
"Forgive them" He prayed.
Be with them in the night
And brightness of eternal day.

THINKING

Think you, I
Anything new
Under the sky?
In the heavens
Upon the earth,
Within a tear,
Sadness, or mirth?
Surly our thoughts
Are nothing new
But to tap new resources,
To get another view;
To mentally reach,
stretch and yawn,
Will take you I know
To a bright new dawn.

Yes, there's something
New under the sky,
It begins with us, you and I.

"Therefore
Be ye
renewed in
mind"

GOD AND COUNTRY

Why have You loved me so and made me who I am
Made me an American and saved me from all harm
Born on this soil, starvation I've never known
And yet I know You did it all, love You have shown.

I am truly am not worthy, by all I know and do,
And yet You said. My love I give all to you.
All that I ha~e known and done, on Thee both I wait.
God and Country together, hold my future fate.

"For God So Loved the World"

BETWEEN POWERS

Beautiful things come out of me,
For beautiful things go in.
Whatever I've acquired in between
Other than the good, defies all
Imaginings in utter awe I've stood.

How can it be this differing,
Struggling back and forth.
Between powers, the powerless stands
With subdued, submissive, open hands.

Watching the good overtake the bad
And the bad overtake the good.
This earth plane knows of struggles lost
and also of struggles won
For beautiful things come out of
Struggles not ended but once begun.

KNOWLEDGE

For Ignorance, no argument can I give.
For Justice, it is slow but sure.
For Peace, after searching is found.
For Love, only One, for God is Eternal.
For Life, love to the fullest,
Moment, by moment.
And then when life is lived
For all its worth, as best as can be,
Return once again to life beyond
Where soul and mind are free.

"life is eternally renewed"

IF I HAD ONLY KNOWN

I would not have offended you had I known
Your vulnerabilities, if you could have shown
Where you hurt, between the pain.
Between the heartache, sorrow and strain.
Where is that part of you gone from my sight?
That you suffered with all through the lonely night?
And if you could tell me, with words you've found,
From within your soul, how would your pain sound?
Let me touch your hidden place, thoughts exposed only to you.
I can help heal the hurt, your soul to finally renew
Itself and come back to me, a point of parting.
Far from darkness, a time of fresh starting.
Free from fear, depression, lost hopes and dreams.
Only then can you know what true life really means,
And begin to live your life renewed,
From a strong foundation that begins with you.

TO PRETEND THE ILLUSION

The time has come when all times must.
. To reassess our values amongst the unjust.
To seek within a profound clearance.
To clear from ourselves the phony pretenses,
That limits our known and unknown senses,
That would allow us to flow free from within
To give a part of the Universe that lies therein.
All that lies without is illusion
To keep you from finding the solution.
Seek within where the answers lie,
You'll be set free before you die.
Ah! but man is hurled forward by all he wants to see
Because there is a time and place for what man shall be.
He struggles endlessly for that timeless ending,
That God, the Universe, and Evolution is sending.
The bowels in me are hard and bitter
At this thing called man, this filth this litter.
Who has lost his place, his heavenly being
Who can only see reality with eyes unseeing.

REFLECTION

I heard the cries of my brother
As I looked into his eyes.
I heard the cries of my brother
And his moaning my heart denies.

What is it to me he is hungry?
What is it to me he is hurt?
Why worry, should he fall?
Why to me does he call?

I hear no cry from his lips.
No call will I ever know.
I am complete within myself,
No love will I ever. show.

I can only believe in self,
And glory in my own growth.
What care I if I can hear,
The moaning of all his fear?

I only know of my tomorrows
And all that that entails.
As for my brother, I only know
From his failure, I set my sails.

For money is what I worship,
And fame I hold so dear.
I know if I have these two,
My first love shall be true.

The world will worship me,
And I will remain on top.
Not caring about another,
His pain I will not stop.

So who am I you say,
To ignore my brother's plea?
Just look into your mirror,
I am the reflection that you see.

A POET'S DILEMMA

How shall I live like a poet, live a poet's fate?
Of blind obedience to the mysteries of love and also hate.
How shall I know the measure of the written word once wrote
To effect the hearts of men with a simple, single stroke.
How much glory of a story written on a Winter's night.
Will I receive as I write by the glow of an overhead light.

I write not for glory, nor fame, nor the recognition of man.
The Poet writes because he's lead by the Great Knowing Hand.

"MAY GOD, THE FATHER BLESS AND KEEP YOU INALL YOUR WAYS AND BRING YOU AND YOURS MANY HAPPY DAYS UPON THE EARTH WHILE NEVER FORGETTING WHOAND WHAT YOU WERE-CREATED FOR; THE SPIRIT IN MAN WAS CREATED TO WOKSHIP AND GROW INTO THE IMAGE AND LIKENESS OF THELIVINGGOD, THE FATHER."

"LOVE AND PEACE;"

Minerva L. Word